A THOUGHT FOR THANKSGIVING

by Norma Minturn Stilwell
Illustrated by Pamela E. Bingham

the Peppertree Press
Sarasota, Florida

This is the first book in the series of *Let's Get Along* books.

Norma Minturn Stilwell is also the author of:
Making Beautiful Music

Copyright © Norma Minturn Stilwell, 2011

All rights reserved. Published by *the* Peppertree Press, LLC.
the Peppertree Press and associated logos are trademarks of
the Peppertree Press, LLC.

No part of this publication may be reproduced, stored in a retrieval system, transmitted in any form or by any means, electronic, mechanical, photocopying, recording, or otherwise, without prior written permission of the publisher and author/illustrator.
Graphic design by Rebecca Barbier.
Illustrations by Pamela E. Bingham

For information regarding permission,
call 941-922-2662 or contact us at our website:
www.peppertreepublishing.com or write to:
the Peppertree Press, LLC.
Attention: Publisher
1269 First Street, Suite 7
Sarasota, Florida 34236

ISBN: 978-1-936343-93-5

Library of Congress Number: 2011929098

Printed in the U.S.A.

Printed June 2011

Dedication

To my grandchildren and children every where to remind them that it is the virtue of tolerance that has made us a great nation.

This book belongs to:

_____

It was powwow time in Plymouth
when the tribes must all convene

to discuss the new arrival of
the pilgrims to the scene.

"I don't like the way they dress" said one Algonquin lad.

"Let's hope those hats and buckled shoes are just a passing fad."

"Who is this god they pray to?"
spoke a tribesman from the Cree.

"He can't be as almighty as the god who cares for me."

"Suppose they kill off all the game" cried an angry Lenape.

"When winter comes I don't know how I'll feed my family."

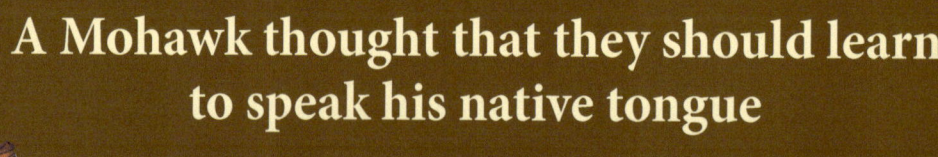

A Mohawk thought that they should learn to speak his native tongue

or board their boat and set their sails
for where they started from.

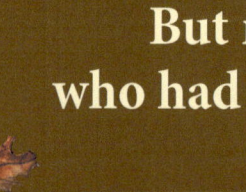

But now the elders of the tribes,
who had reached some three score years,

spoke with aged wisdom
to calm their tribesmen's fears.

15

"All our tribes are different none exactly like the other.

Let's give our hand in friendship to our white skinned brother."

"We'll teach him how to hunt and fish and plant his fields with corn."

We'll show him how to sew up hides to keep his family warm."

"And when the harvesting is done and summer turns to fall,

we'll join with him in giving thanks
to the god who loves us all."

THE END

GLOSSARY

Algonquin - A North American Indian tribe

Convene - To come together for a purpose

Cree - A North American Indian tribe

Fad - A short lived popular fashion

Lenape - A North American Indian tribe

Mohawk - A North American Indian tribe

Powwow - A meeting of Native Americans

Three score years - A score is equal to twenty years, so three score would equal sixty years

www.ingramcontent.com/pod-product-compliance
Ingram Content Group UK Ltd.
Pitfield, Milton Keynes, MK11 3LW, UK
UKHW060137240426

12048UKWH00002B/81